LATE HAVE I LOVED YOU

MARIAROSA GUERRINI O.S.A.

LATE HAVE I LOVED YOU

ST AUGUSTINE
a man of God...
a man for others...

sp St Paul Publications

Original title: TARDI TI AMAI. Produced by the Federation of Augustinian Nuns, Italy, and first published in 1983 by Editrice Rogate, Rome. Fourth reprint 1985. All rights reserved.

English language edition:

Texts from the **Confessions** (marked in this book simply by a reference number, e.g.: 10,6) are taken from **St Augustine, Confessions**, translated by R.S. Pine-Coffin (Penguin Classics, 1961) copyright © R.S. Pine-Coffin 1961. Reproduced by permission of Penguin Books Ltd.

Other texts translated by Vincent Siletti SSP
Text lettering by Mary Lou Winters DSP

St Paul Publications
Middlegreen, Slough SL3 6BT, England

English language edition copyright
© St Paul Publications 1986
Published in June 1986
Printed by Billing & Sons, Worcester
ISBN 085439 252 1

WE ALL NEED
      SOMEONE
TO WHOM WE CAN RELATE
WITH OUR HUMAN EXPERIENCE.

WE ALL NEED
      SOMEONE
WHO SHOWS US THE WAY
TO FIND OUR TRUE SELVES.

WE ALL NEED
      SOMEONE
WHO GOES BEFORE US
IN THE STUPENDOUS
AND ARDUOUS WAYS OF GOD.

ST AUGUSTINE
HAS BEEN FOR US
THIS SOMEONE.

We have thought of offering to many others
the possibility and joy
of meeting him along this life's journey,
but in a simple, smiling manner.

St Augustine will be pleased
because he was the first
to spend years and years
breaking bread to his simple faithful
−the fresh bread of the Word,
the Word who turned him into a new being.

THE AUGUSTINIAN NUNS

CONTENTS

YOUR WORD
STRUCK
INTO MY HEART
AND FROM THAT
MOMENT
I LOVED YOU...!

10,6

9

A TROUBLED HEART

You made us
for yourself
and our hearts
find no peace
until they
rest in you.

1,1

BEAUTY
at once so ancient and so new
I have learnt to love
you late!

10, 27

You were within me,
and I was in the world outside myself.
I searched for you...
You were within me,
but I was not with you.

You called me.
You cried aloud to me.
You broke the barrier of my deafness.

You shone upon me,
Your radiance enveloped me,
You put my blindness to flight.

You shed your fragrance about me;
I drew breath and now
I gasp for your sweet odour.

You touched me,
and I am inflamed
with love of your peace.

10, 27

11

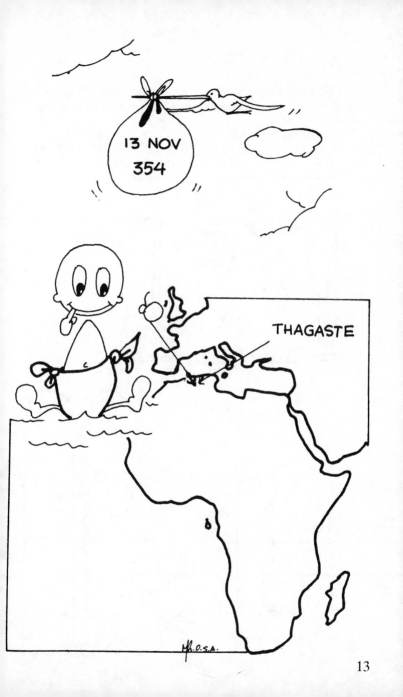

13

MY PARENTS

Patricius, my father, was a pagan. Though he was remarkably kind, he had a hot temper. 9,9

Monica, my mother, was a Christian. She had a strong faith, the composure of her years, and a mother's love for her son.

9,4

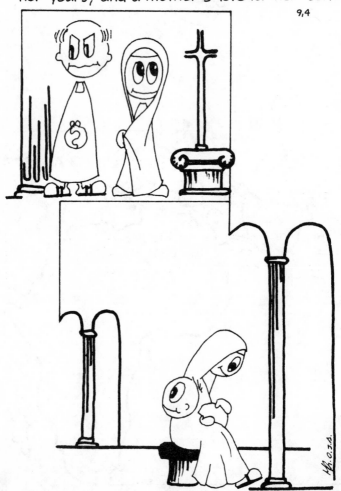

THE SEED OF FAITH
WILL GROW

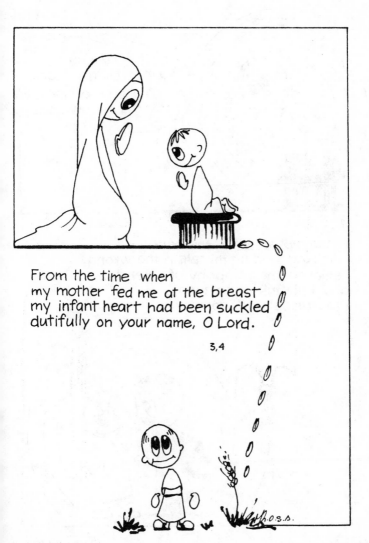

From the time when
my mother fed me at the breast
my infant heart had been suckled
dutifully on your name, O Lord.

3,4

LITTLE BOY AUGUSTINE

I found pleasure in the truth.
I disliked finding myself in the wrong.
I enjoyed the company of friends;
and I shrank from pain,
ignorance and sorrow.

1, 20

ALLUREMENT

...But I did not love you.
I broke my troth with you
and embraced another,
with applause echoed about me.

1, 13

I drifted farther and farther away from you.
I was so blind to the truth
that among my companions I was ashamed
to be less dissolute than they were.

2, 3

PRIDE

In the games I played I often cheated
in order to come off the better
simply because a vain desire to win
had got the better of me. 1, 19

My sin was this, that I looked for
pleasure, beauty, and truth
not in Him, but in myself and
His other creatures. 1, 20

A PASSION FOR THE THEATRE

I was much attracted to the theatre, because the plays reflected my own unhappy plight and were tinder to my fire.

3,2

HONOURS AND.....

Besides these pursuits I was also studying for the law. Such ambition was held to be honourable. The more unscrupulous I was, the greater my reputation was likely to be, for men are so blind that they even take pride in their blindness.

3.3

I was at the top of the school of rhetoric.
I was pleased with my superior status and swollen with conceit.

3.3

It was my ambition to be a good speaker for the unhallowed and inane purpose of gratifying human vanity.

3.4

LOVE AND.....

I had not yet fallen in love,
but I was in love with the idea of it.
I began to look around for some
object for my love,
since I badly wanted to love something.

TO LOVE AND TO HAVE MY LOVE RETURNED
WAS MY HEART'S DESIRE.

3.1

..... PASSION

In those days I lived with a woman, not my lawful wedded wife but a mistress whom I had chosen for no special reason but that my restless passion had alighted on her. But she was the only one and I was faithful to her.

Living with her I found out by my own experience the difference between the restraint of the marriage alliance contracted for the purpose of having children, and a bargain struck for lust, in which the birth of children is to be grudged, though, if they come, we cannot help but love them.

4,2

23

MY REARING PRIDE

Mistaken ideas and false
beliefs will poison life,
if the rational mind is
corrupt...
and in those days
my mind was corrupt...
but...

You thrust me back and crushed my rearing pride.
I drifted on, making my way towards things
that had no existence in you... they were not
created for me by your truth but were the
inventions of my own foolish imagination
working on material things...

4.15

...I did not know that if
it was to share in the truth,
it must be illumined by
another light, because the mind
itself is not the essence of truth.

It is you, O Lord that keep
the lamp of my hopes still burning.

4,15

WHEN I WAS 19
(A.D. 373)

At that impressionable age...
a book altered my outlook on life.
It changed my prayers to you, O Lord,
and provided me with new hopes
and aspirations.
All my empty dreams suddenly lost
their charm and my heart
began to throb with bewildering
passion for the wisdom of eternal truth.

3.4

I BEGAN TO CLIMB OUT OF THE DEPTHS TO RETURN TO YOU

THE FIRST APPROACHES

The words of that book...
excited me and set me burning with fire,
and the only check to this blaze
of enthusiasm was that they made
no mention of the name of Christ.

Nothing could entirely captivate me,
unless his name were in it.
3,4

So I made up my mind
to examine the holy Scriptures
and see what kind of books
they were...
3,3

A DELUSION

I discovered something that was at once
beyond the understanding of the proud
and hidden from the eyes of children.
It was enfolded in mysteries,
and I was not the kind of man to enter into it
and bow my head to follow where it led.

I had too much conceit to accept
their simplicity and not enough
insight to penetrate their depths.
It is surely true that as the child grows
these books grow with him.
But I was too proud to call myself
a child. I was inflated with
self-esteem, which made me think of
myself as a great man.

3.5

TOWARDS OTHER DECEPTIONS

I fell in with a set of sensualists,
men with glib tongues
who ranted and raved
and had the snares of the devil
in their mouths—
the Manichees.

'Truth and truth alone',
they repeated to me again and again,
although the truth was nowhere
to be found in them.

3.6

WHERE WERE YOU ?...!...?

Where were you in those days?
How far away from me?

These were the stages
of my pitfall into the depths of hell,
as I struggled and strained
for lack of the truth...
3.6

33

LEADING AND LED ASTRAY

From the nineteenth to the twenty-eighth
year of my life, I was led astray myself
and led others astray in my turn.
We were deceivers and deceived in all our
different aims and ambitions...
We would hunt for worthless popular
distinctions...
for quickly fading wreaths won in competition.

In public we were cocksure,
in private superstitious,
and everywhere void and empty.
In self indulgence
we were unrestrained.

4,1

Nothing would ever prevent me from consulting those imposters... whom they called astrologers.
4,3

A DREAM

My mother wept to you for me.
For in her faith she looked on me as dead.
You heard her and did not despise her tears.

She dreamed that she was standing on a wooden rule,
and coming towards her in a halo of splendour she saw
a young man who smiled at her in joy, although she
herself was sad and quite consumed with grief.
He asked her the reason for her sorrow... he told
her to take heart for, if she looked carefully
she would see that where she was,
there also was I. And when she looked,
she saw me standing beside her
on the same rule.

3. 11

THE SON OF SO MANY TEARS

My mother asked a certain bishop,
as a favour,
to have a talk with me...

'Go in peace', he said. 'It cannot be
that the son of these tears should be lost'.

3, 12

THE DEATH OF A FRIEND

During those years I had found a very dear friend. There was a sweetness in our friendship, mellowed by the interests we shared. I had drawn him away from the true faith to believe in the same superstitions, self-destroying fallacies which brought my mother to tears over me.

He was my companion in error and I was utterly lost without him.

Yet, in a moment...
you took him from this world.

My heart grew sombre with grief and wherever I looked I saw only death.

4.4

LIFE BEGINS ANEW

Time never stands still,
nor does it idly pass without effect
upon our feelings. My greatest
comfort and relief was in the solace
of other friends... We could talk and
laugh together and exchange small
acts of kindness...
We could be grave or light-hearted.

Each of us had something
to learn from the others
and something to teach in return
If any were away,
we missed them with regret,
and gladly welcomed them
when they came home.

4.8

FRIENDSHIP IS.....

Blessed are those who love you, O God,
and love their friends in you
and their enemies for your sake.
They alone will never lose those
who are dear to them,
for they love them in One who is never lost.
4.9

..... BLESSEDNESS!

DISAPPOINTED

For almost nine years
I waited the coming
of this man Faustus (a Manichean bishop)
with keenest expectation.
5,6

At last he arrived.
Those who had given me assurance about him
must have been poor judges.
As soon as it became clear to me
that Faustus was quite uninformed
about the subjects in which I had expected
him to be an expert, I began to lose hope
that he could lift the veil and resolve
the problems which perplexed me.

5,6,7

I made up my mind
to leave the Manichees.
5,19

GOD.............KEPT WATCH

In the mystery of your providence,
my God, your guiding hand
did not desert me.
Night and day my mother poured
out her tears to you and offered
her heart-blood in sacrifice for me,
and in the most wonderful way
you guided me.
5,7

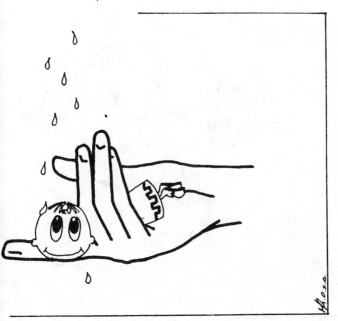

FROM CARTHAGE TO.....

Secretly, I sailed away...
leaving my mother alone
in her tears and in her prayers.

5,8

A DISAPPOINTED TEACHER!

IN MILAN

As I walked along one of the streets,
I noticed a poor beggar who must, I suppose,
have had his fill of food and drink since he was
laughing and joking. Sadly I turned to my
companions and spoke to them
of all the pain and trouble which is
caused by our folly.
The only purpose of all the efforts
we made was to reach the goal
of peaceful happiness...
which this beggar had already
reached ahead of us,
and which perhaps we
should never reach at all.

6.6

A PROJECT

A group of my friends who detested the bustle and worry of life had all but decided to live a life of peace away from the crowd. We had thought over this project. The plan was to arrange this life of leisure by pooling our possessions and using such money as we had between us to create a common fund. In the spirit of sincere friendship none of us would claim this or that as his own.

But when we began to ask ourselves whether the women would agree to this plan, all our carefully made arrangements collapsed and broke to pieces in our hands and were discarded.

6.14

OUR HEARTS.....

It was a constant subject of talk among my circle of friends, but I used to discuss it especially with Alypius and Nebridius.
6,7

..... WERE HUNGRY!

We were like three hungry mouths,
able to gasp out our needs
to one another,
while our eyes were on you, O Lord,
waiting for you to grant us,
in due time, our nourishment.

6,10

MY HEART WAS RENT

I was being urged incessantly to marry
and had already made my proposal
and been accepted.

The woman with whom I had been living
was torn away from my side as an
obstacle to my marriage and this was
a blow which crushed my heart to
bleeding because I loved her dearly.

She went back to Africa,
and left me with
the son whom she had borne me.

52

CONTINUING...
ALONG CROOKED PATHS

I was impatient at the delay
of two years which had
to pass before the girl whom
I had asked to marry became
my wife, and I took another
mistress without the sanction of wedlock.
6,15

ASTROLOGY ?..!..?

By this time I had also turned my back
upon the astrologers with their
illusory claims to predict the future.
There is no art by which the future
can be foretold; guesswork is often
borne out by mere chance.

7.6

EVIL ?..!..?

Where is evil?
What is its origin?
How did it steal into the world?
What is the root or seed from which it grew?
7,5

RESPONSIBILITY
LIES WITH THE PERSON

These were the thoughts
which I turned over and over .
in my unhappy mind, and any anxiety
was all the more galling for the fear
that death might come before
I had found the truth.

7,5

A DECISIVE READING

Certain books served me to return
to my own self. Under your
guidance I entered the depths of
my soul.

I saw the Light that
never changes casting
its rays over the same
eye of my soul.
It shone above my mind.
All who know the truth
know this Light,
and all who know this Light
know eternity.
It is the Light that love knows.

I heard your voice,
as we hear voices
that speak to our hearts,
and at once I had no cause
to doubt.

7.10 .

ETERNAL TRUTH
TRUE LOVE
BELOVED ETERNITY

All this, my God, you are,
and it is to you that
I sigh by night and day.

7, 10

RISE.....

I was astonished that although I now loved you and not some phantom in your place, I did not persist in enjoyment of my God.

Your beauty drew me to you...

..... AND FALL

...but soon I was dragged away from you by my own weight and in dismay I plunged again into the things of this world.

7,17

IN SEARCH OF COURAGE

I began to search for a means
of gaining the strength I needed...
7, 18

I seized eagerly upon the
venerable writings inspired by
your Holy Spirit,
especially those
of the apostle Paul.
7, 21

BUT STILL I HELD BACK

I should have been glad to follow
the right road
to follow the Saviour himself,
but still I could not make up
my mind to venture
along the narrow path.
I was still held firm
in the bonds of a woman's love.

8,1

STRUGGLE

Two wills within me,
one old, one new,
one the servant of the flesh,
the other of the spirit,
were in conflict and between them
they tore my soul apart.
8,5

LOOKING FOR HELP

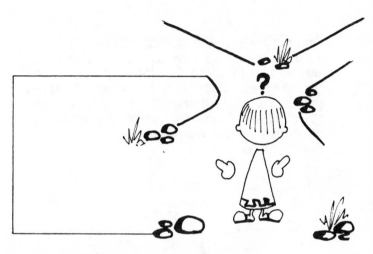

I went to Simplicianus.
To encourage me to follow Christ's example of
humility, he told me the story of Victorinus - an old man
of great learning . . .
who was not
ashamed to be the
child of Christ.
I began to glow with
fervour to imitate him.

8, 2-8, 5

DISCOVERY OF THE BEAUTY OF THE MONASTIC LIFE

One day we were visited at our home
by a man named Ponticianus. When I told
him that I studied Paul's writings with
the greatest attention, he began to tell us
the story of Anthony, the Egyptian monk...
Then he went on to tell us of the groups
of monks in the monasteries and of
their way of life.

8,6

ENCOUNTER
WITH ONESELF

You were turning me around to look
at myself, O Lord. For I had placed
myself behind my own back,
refusing to see myself...

You brought me face to face
with myself once more,
forcing me upon my own sight
so that I should see my wickedness
and loathe it.
8.7

In the heart of the fierce conflict
which I had stirred up against
my soul in our common abode,
my heart, I turned to Alypius.

'These men have not had
our schooling,
yet they stand up
and storm the
gates of heaven
while we,
for all our learning,
lie here grovelling in this
world of flesh
and blood!'
8.8

A DELUGE OF TEARS

I probed the hidden depths of my soul
and wrung its pitiful secrets from it,
and when I mustered them all
before the eyes of my heart,
a great storm broke within me,
bringing with it a deluge of tears...

'How long shall I go on saying "tomorrow, tomorrow"?
why not now?'

8,12

I was asking myself these questions,
weeping all the while
with the most bitter sorrow in my heart,
when all at once I heard the sing-song
voice of a child in a nearby house. 8,12

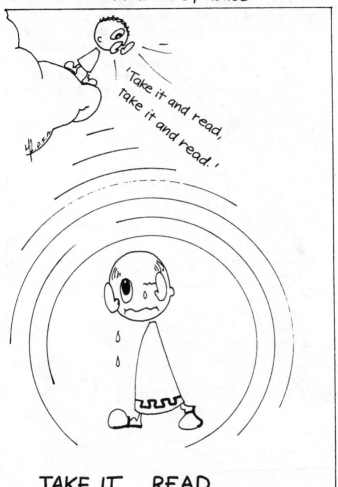

.....TAKE IT...READ.....

CONVERSION

I seized the book containing Paul's Epistles,
and opened it, and in silence I read:

> *Not in revelling and drunkenness,*
> *not in lust and wantonness,*
> *not in quarrels and rivalries.*
> *Rather, arm yourselves*
> *with the Lord Jesus Christ'.*

You converted me to yourself
so that I no longer desired a wife
or placed any hope in this world.

8,12

MY MOTHER'S JOY

I closed the book.
I told Alypius what had happened to me.
Then we went in and told my mother.
When we described how it had all happened,
she was overjoyed,
jubilant with triumph and glorified you.

8,12

AT THE SERVICE OF CHRIST

You had pierced
our hearts.
9,2

I notified the people of Milan
that they must find another
vendor of words for their students,
because
I HAD CHOSEN TO BE YOUR SERVANT.
9.5

Your word struck into my heart
and from that moment I loved you.

Besides this, all about me,
heaven and earth and all that they contain,
proclaim that I should love you.

10,6

AND NOW
YOU ALONE I LOVE
YOU ALONE I FOLLOW
YOU ALONE I SEEK

Soliloquies 1,1

BUT WHAT DO I LOVE
WHEN I LOVE MY GOD?

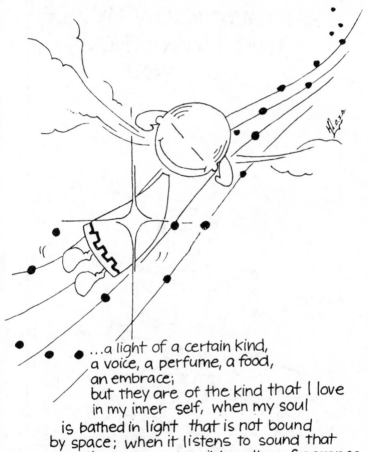

...a light of a certain kind,
a voice, a perfume, a food,
an embrace;
but they are of the kind that I love
in my inner self, when my soul
is bathed in light that is not bound
by space; when it listens to sound that
never dies away; when it breathes fragrance
that is never consumed by the eating;
when it clings to an embrace from which it is
not severed by fulfillment of desire.
This is what I love when I love my God.

10,6

THAT I MAY KNOW MYSELF
THAT I MAY KNOW
YOU

Soliloquies 2,1

REBORN
(A.D. 387)

My brothers and sisters,
children of the catholic Church,
born from on high
and reborn in Christ,
give ear to my word;
sing for me
A NEW SONG.....

DISCOURSE 34

It was Alypius's wish
to be reborn in you at the same time.
We were baptized, and all anxiety
over the past melted away from us.
9,6

NOSTALGIA

Tears flowed from me when I heard
your hymns and canticles,
for the sweet singing of your Church
moved me deeply.
The music surged in my ears,
truth seeped into my heart,
and my feelings of devotion overflowed,
so that the tears streamed down.
But they were tears of gladness.

9,6

WITH HIS MOTHER
FINALLY.............IN GOD!

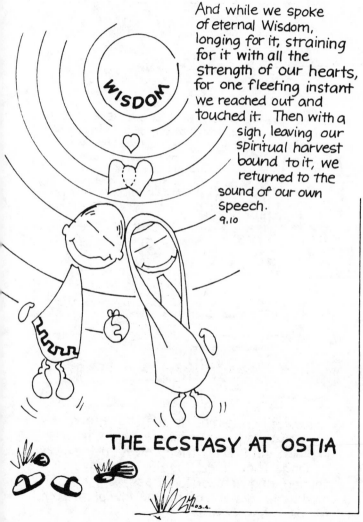

And while we spoke of eternal Wisdom, longing for it, straining for it with all the strength of our hearts, for one fleeting instant we reached out and touched it. Then with a sigh, leaving our spiritual harvest bound to it, we returned to the sound of our own speech.

9.10

THE ECSTASY AT OSTIA

THAGASTE (A.D. 388)
MONASTIC LIFE

All those who believed were of ONE HEART AND SOUL, and no one said that any of the things which he possessed was his own, but they had everything in common.
... they devoted themselves to fellowship, to the breaking of bread, and to prayer.

Acts of the Apostles.

After his baptism he decided to return to Africa, to his own house, with friends who, like him, had given themselves to the service of God. They lived together in prayer, fasting, and acts of kindness, meditating day and night the law of the Lord.

Possidius : Life of St Augustine

ONE HEART
ONE SOUL

Communitarian love
turned many souls
into one soul
many hearts
into one heart.

commentary on John 14, 9

SEARCHING FOR GOD TOGETHER

Why do you wish that those who are dear to you stay and live together with you?

> So that we may search into God and our soul in collaboration and with unanimous will. It will then be easier for the one who has been first to find God to help others in their search.

SOLILOQUIES 1, 12

THE COMMUNITY IS THE HOUSE OF GOD

They will not, however,
be the House of God
until they are bound together in love.

If these beams, these stones
do not adhere to one another
in some kind of order,
if they do not harmonically connect,
no one will enter this House.

DISCOURSE 236

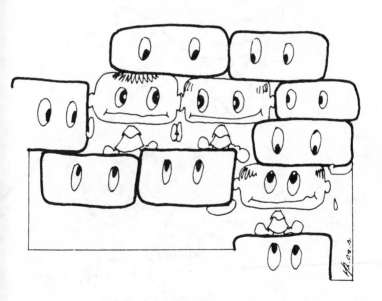

HOW GOOD
HOW PLEASANT IT IS

when brothers dwell
in unity

It is like the dew
of Hermon
which falls on
the mountains of Sion...
PSALM 132

82

These words,
this gentle harmony,
this sweet melody,
thought out in the heart
and spoken in song
have given birth to Monasteries.

It was this harmony,
this melody, that awakened
in the Brothers their desire
to live in unity
and brought it to maturity.

This verse
was for them like a trumpet:
it blared and, behold,
it gathered people
who had until then
been scattered all over the world.

The divine cry,
the cry of the Holy Spirit,
the cry of prophecy,
that was not heard in Judaea,
has been heard throughout the world.

EXPOSITION OF PSALM 132

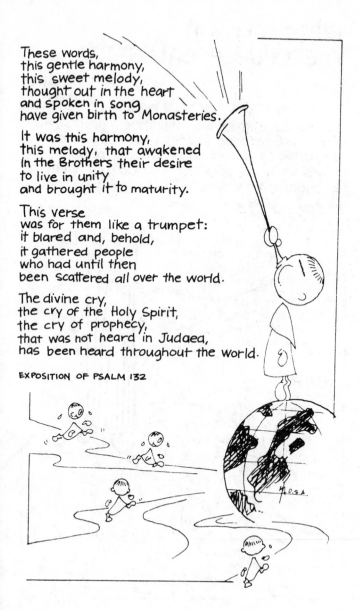

HIPPO (A.D. 391)
THE CHURCH CALLS

His friend Possidius wrote:

'The catholics who knew Augustine's programme
of life and doctrine imposed hands on him
so that the bishop would ordain him priest.
He was unaware of what was about to happen.
He cried and cried, but... it happened.'

POSSIDIUS: LIFE OF St AUGUSTINE

I looked for a place where
to found a Monastery
to live in community
with my friends,
... and they
made me accept
being ordained
priest.

DISCOURSE 365

HELP!

ALSO AT HIPPO:
MONASTIC LIFE

After his ordination, he founded a Monastery and went to live there with the 'servants of God' following the Rule established by the Apostles:

EVERYTHING WAS TO BE HELD IN COMMON

POSSIDIUS: LIFE OF ST AUGUSTINE

LISTENING
TO THE WORD OF GOD

You made me a preacher of your Word. I burn with desire to contemplate your law. I do not wish to allow my time to slip away by undertaking any other task when I am free from the necessities of giving service to others.

11,2

Let your Scriptures
be my chaste delight.
Let me not deceive myself in them
nor deceive others about them.

11, 2

Your voice is my joy,
a greater joy than any profusion
of worldly pleasures.
Do not abandon what you have given me.
Do not scorn what you have planted
when it is parched with thirst for you.

Let me listen to the sound of your praises.
Let me drink you in
and contemplate the wonders of your law.

11, 2

UNTIRING MINISTRY

All that God revealed to him in meditation and prayer he shared with those who were near and those who were far with discourses and books.

POSSIDIUS : LIFE OF ST AUGUSTINE

BISHOP (A.D. 395)

The lamp,
alight and brightly burning,
placed on a stand,
shed its light on all those
who were in the house.

POSSIDIUS: LIFE OF ST AUGUSTINE

THE IDEAL
OF MONASTIC LIFE
KEEPS ON

Having been ordained bishop
I wanted to have with me
a monastery of clerics.

DISCOURSE: 355

SIMPLICITY OF LIFE
...AND FREEDOM
OF THE SPIRIT

In his clothes, in his bedroom,
there was moderation and dignity;
he avoided refinements
as he avoided slovenliness.

POSSIDIUS: LIFE OF ST AUGUSTINE

CHARITY ABOVE ALL

He always practised hospitality.
When at table he preferred listening
to the reading, or conversation,
to the food and drink.

HE WHO SPEAKS ILL
OF THOSE WHO ARE ABSENT
IS NOT WORTHY
TO SIT AT THIS TABLE.

POSSIDIUS: LIFE OF ST AUGUSTINE

REVIVING
THE CHURCH

Augustine taught and preached
at home and in church,
and the catholic Church of Africa
regained vitality.

POSSIDIUS: LIFE OF ST AUGUSTINE

HE WRITES
THE CITY OF GOD

Rome was attacked with sword and fire by the Goths. The pagans attributed this to the Christian religion.

Burning with zeal for the House of the Lord, I decided to write THE CITY OF GOD against such insults...

RETRACTATIONS 2

NOSTALGIA FOR...

Love of the truth
seeks the silence of
contemplation,...

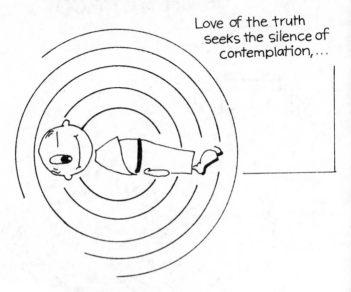

... the duty of love
accepts the
activity of the apostolate.
THE CITY OF GOD 19,19

He wrote to the nuns
of a monastery he had founded:
'I rejoice thinking of you
-in this world full of scandals.
In you I find consolation:
thinking of your union,
of your holy love.
Thinking of the gifts
that the Lord has given you,
my heart finds rest.'

LETTER 211

HIPPO UNDER SIEGE

We must not abandon the Church
that we have been called to serve if,
where we are, there are still
even only a few of the people of God.

LETTER 228

HIS DEATH
(28 AUGUST 430)

During his illness,
upon his bed,
his eyes were fixed on the psalms of David:
he read them,
he wept,
he prayed...
... and so he fell asleep.

POSSIDIUS : LIFE OF ST AUGUSTINE

ALL THE WORLD CAME TO KNOW HIM

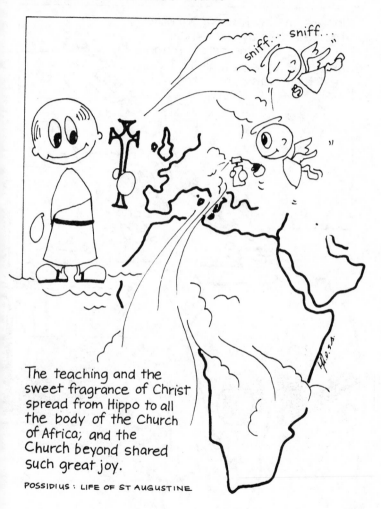

The teaching and the sweet fragrance of Christ spread from Hippo to all the body of the Church of Africa; and the Church beyond shared such great joy.

POSSIDIUS : LIFE OF ST AUGUSTINE

SPREADING ABROAD

Incursions by the barbarians tried to destroy monastic life in Africa, but the persecution and exile spread it all the more and transplanted it abroad.

MONASTIC RULE
OF
ST AUGUSTINE

MANY HAVE BEEN
THE MEN AND WOMEN
WHO CONSECRATED THEMSELVES TO GOD
IN THE MONASTIC LIFE
FOUNDED BY ST AUGUSTINE.

TODAY THERE ARE STILL
MANY AUGUSTINIAN MONKS AND NUNS
WHO SHARE AND WANT TO COMMUNICATE
TO OTHERS HIS YEARNING FOR GOD
AND HIS EAGERNESS FOR THE
SALVATION OF ALL.

THE FOLLOWING PAGES,
CONTAINING PASSAGES FROM
THE MONASTIC RULE OF ST AUGUSTINE,
ARE MEANT TO GIVE A GLIMPSE
OF THEIR WAY OF LIFE.

1. Brothers, love God with all your heart, and your neighbour too, for this is what God wants from you, above all else.

2. You are to observe the precepts that follow; they are necessary for an orderly life in the monastic community.

BE OF ONE MIND AND HEART

3. The reason why you have come to live together is to search for God untiringly; therefore, live in harmony of mind and heart.

4. In the monastic community nobody should say that anything he has belongs to him; everything is to be shared in common.

5. Those who owned possessions should readily agree that once they enter the monastery all becomes property of the community.

6. Those who come from a lower class should not expect from the community what they did not have before entering the monastery.

HUMILITY:
ESSENTIAL FOR MONASTIC LIFE

7. No one should feel proud to live in the monastic community together with people whom they would not otherwise have been able to associate with. Rather, their hearts should seek more noble things.

8. Those who thought they had some high status in society should not feel ill at ease to live together with Brothers who come from a lower class; in fact, they should see it as a blessing.

EXHORTATION
To LIVE IN HARMONY

9. Live, therefore, in harmony; and honour God in one another, because you are temples of the living God.

PRAYER

10. Persevere in prayer. Be faithful to the hours and for the time appointed.

11. The place for prayer should be used for that purpose only; so that, if someone wants to pray there alone, outside the appointed hours, he will not be prevented from doing so.

12. When you pray with the words of the Psalms or with hymns, let your lips speak the expressions of your heart.

13. And when you sing, follow all the instructions. Do not sing as you please or what is not meant to be sung.

FASTING AND ABSTINENCE

14. Taking care of your health, keep your passions and desires under control by fasting and abstinence.

READING DURING MEALS

15. From the beginning of the meal to the end, listen attentively to what is being read.

CARE FOR THE WEAK

16. Any exception made for those who are weaker to have adequate food should not be seen as unfair by those who are stronger.

AUSTERITY
AND UNDERSTANDING

17. No one should expect to receive that which is given to some by way of exception, for this is done not because of any privilege but out of concern.

CONCERN FOR THE SICK

18. The sick naturally eat less during their illness; therefore, during their convalescence they should be treated in a way that they can make a quick recovery.

THE DRESS

19. Let it be simple.
Do your best not to attract attention
by the way you dress but, rather,
to give witness by your manner of life.

WHEN OUTSIDE
THE MONASTERY

20. When you have to go out,
go with somebody else from the
community and always keep together.

21. In all that you say or do you should
never give offence to anyone.
Your behaviour should reveal at all
times the holiness of your life.

22. Wherever you may be, you are to watch over one another's chastity. The Lord who dwells in you will watch over you through this kind of attention you give to one another.

CAUTIONARY ADVICE

23. If a Brother has done something wrong, you must point it out to him, so that evil may not take root in him and gain a stronger hold in his heart.

24. If a Brother will not listen to you and takes no step in correcting his error, you have to inform the community, but first advise the Superior so that he may caution the Brother in private and others will not need to know about it.

LOVE PEOPLE
HATE EVIL

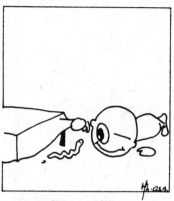

25. It must be with great care and concern that you prevent, point out or correct errors, and if necessary punish; but do so in private.

26. If one of you has gone so far in the ways of evil as to receive letters or gifts secretly, but freely confesses this wrong, then he is to be forgiven, and everyone should pray for him.

123

CLOTHES
FROM ONE WARDROBE

27. Clothes are to be kept in a common wardrobe
and to be looked after by one or more
Brothers. All the clothes you wear are
to come from the one and only wardrobe.

EVERYTHING FOR THE GOOD OF THE COMMUNITY

28. Whatsoever you do is done not for yourself but for the whole community; and your enthusiasm should be all the greater precisely because it is for the good of all.

29. Everything you receive should be handed over to the Superior for the good of the community. The Superior will dispose of it according to the needs.

30. The Superior will decide on all matters concerning your clothes, so that no vanity will endanger your soul.

IN SICKNESS

31. If one of you needs to go to the public
baths, permission should be given;
and there should be no grumbling.
If one of you is sick, he must obey
doctor's orders, and do everything
necessary to regain his health.

32. When a Brother
complains of some
illness or pain not
noticeable by others,
he is to be believed
without hesitation.

GOING OUT TOGETHER

33. Do not go out, anywhere, alone.
The Brothers you go out with are
to be chosen by the Superior,
you cannot choose them yourself.

THE SERVICE OF LOVE

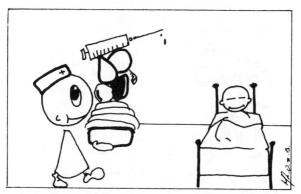

34. Care of the sick, of those convalescing, of those suffering from minor ailments, is to be entrusted to one of the Brothers who will obtain from the common store all that is necessary for each individual person.

35. Those in charge of the kitchen, the library, the wardrobe, should give their service to the Brothers with care and joy.

36. Books should be requested on a daily basis only, and at the appointed hours. No book should be given to anyone outside those hours.

37. But the Brothers in charge should at once give clothes and shoes to anyone who needs them.

RECIPROCAL FORGIVENESS

38. There should never be a quarrel among you; but if it should happen then break it up at once, because anger easily makes a log out of a speck and turns one's heart to murderous feelings.

39. A Brother who has no intention of asking
forgiveness or does not do so of his own
free will and wholeheartedly should
leave the monastery, even if he has not
been turned away.

THE SERVICE OF AUTHORITY

40. When, for motives of discipline, the Superior speaks hard words to admonish and correct the Brothers, though it may be that he has gone too far, he is not bound to apologise to those under his authority.

41. Obey your Superior as you would obey your father, with the honour due to him. For obedience to him is obedience to God.

42. It is the duty of the Superior to see to it that all these precepts are kept. If any of them has been transgressed, he should not let it go without appropriate correction.

43. The Superior should not be proud of his position of authority; rather, he should be happy to be of greater service to the community. He holds authority over the Brothers so that they may honour God through their obedience; but he is to serve the Brothers so that he may not fall into any sin of pride.

44. Obey willingly and with enthusiasm, so that you may obtain mercy for yourselves and also for him who, being in authority, is exposed to greater dangers.

FINAL EXHORTATION

45. May the Lord give you grace to observe this Rule with love, love for its inner beauty. Let your holiness of life exhale the sweet fragrance of Jesus Christ, not as subjects of the law but as children of grace.

REVISION OF LIFE

46. Read this little book once a week
to see yourself as in a mirror.

ST AUGUSTINE
was the first one of us
to have been pursued and seized by God...
Following his conversion
he surrendered himself entirely to Him
who is ... Beauty...Wisdom...Truth...Love!

And we too,
like St Augustine,
together

SEEK THE FACE OF GOD

MONASTIC LIFE OF THE NUNS.....TODAY

All those who believed were of ONE HEART AND SOUL, and no one said that any of the things which he possessed was his own, but they had everything in common.

ACTS OF THE APOSTLES.

The above words explain who we are- AUGUSTINIAN NUNS in the contemplative life.

The experience of those early Christians has seized us too and completely immersed us in an adventure that we ourselves are unable to describe... It has brought us together, here, yes, into a Cloister, in order to place us in the infinite space of God and into the heart of men and women of our times.

CLOISTER?

SEARCHING FOR GOD
SEARCHING FOR MAN
BY WAY OF THE HEART

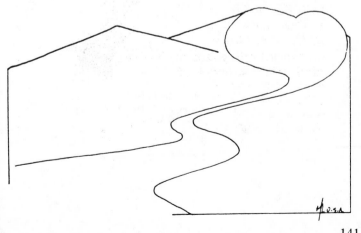

Searching for God
we discover,
to our surprise and joy,
that the surest way to be
in communion with all men and women,
with all created beings,
is by way of the heart.

Our heart
is for us the open space
of sublime, all embracing love,
because God lives in our hearts
and He is love.

How wonderful it is
to seek THE TRUTH together,
to go deep into the Truth...
We come to maturity,
we learn to dialogue,
we look with a sense of responsibility
into the problems that afflict
our brothers and sisters in the world
outside the Cloister.

THE WORD OF GOD
guides our way of life,
our heart,
our daily activities.

THE WORD OF GOD
gives light to our mind

probes our heart

reveals
GOD'S PLAN
for each one of us.

A WHOLE LIFE
LISTENING TO THE WORD OF GOD

COMMENTARY ON ST JOHN

In recollection and stillness
we have communion with Him,
in a mystery of light and joy.

God and man
have but one desire:
TO MEET

Those who are
faithful to Him
find rest in love,
having been called
from the tumult
of this world
to the joys of
silence and
peace.

ON THE TRINITY

EXPOSITION OF PSALM 37

Prayer
is a dialogue, an existence,
a life that is a continuous
PRAISE OF GOD.

Praying together
is at the centre of all our life
and it marks the hours of our day.

I consecrate myself to God for all the days of my life taking the vows of poverty, chastity and obedience, and I promise to live fully the life in common with the Sisters, seeking God and serving the Church.

AUGUSTINIAN RITUAL

Our whole life cries out:

GO BACK TO YOUR HEART
GO BACK TO YOURSELF
GO BACK TO GOD

This is the simple, crystal-clear message
of St Augustine,
who had the sorrowful experience
of a long wandering
outside of himself.

...GO BACK
TO YOUR HEART!

My heart is my whole being.
It is the "secret room"
that guards my identity,
where I am truly myself,
where my life story unfolds.

Outside of my heart
I am lost.
And there in its silent depths,
I can see THE FACE OF GOD
....whom I seek,
for whom my heart is yearning.

Publisher's note

This little book
has been produced
and published by
the priests and brothers
of the Society of St Paul
and the Daughters of St Paul,
two of the Congregations of
the Pauline Family whose mission
is to proclaim the Gospel
all over the world
through the media of
social communication.

Have you read:

DO YOU LOVE ME?

A GENIAL WAY OF
PRESENTING THE GOSPEL....

THE CALL OF THE GOSPEL
AND PETER'S RESPONSE OF LOVE
ILLUSTRATED WITH
AN ADMIRABLE SENSE OF HUMOUR....

The fascinating adventure of following Jesus and the sweeping message of his teaching are, here, narrated by Peter, the apostle who experienced the unutterable joy of the answer to the call of the Lord.

Peter's is the story of impassioned love — unique. Reading its pages, everyone will be able to grasp the criterion and the measure of true and real love.

Next: